✱ SAVE THE ✱
EVERGLADES

by Judith Bauer Stamper

Alex Haley, General Editor

Illustrations by Allen Davis

RSVP
RAINTREE
STECK-VAUGHN
P U B L I S H E R S
The Steck-Vaughn Company

Austin, Texas

To Gwen

Published by Steck-Vaughn Company.

Text, illustrations, and cover art copyright © 1993 by Dialogue
Systems, Inc., 627 Broadway, New York, New York 10012.
All rights reserved.

Cover art by Allen Davis

Printed in the United States of America
3 4 5 6 7 8 9 R 98 97 96

Library of Congress Cataloging-in-Publication Data
Stamper, Judith Bauer.
    Save the Everglades/Judith Bauer Stamper; illustrator, Allen Davis.
      p. cm.—(Stories of America)
    Summary: Describes the successful efforts of concerned citizens to
stop construction of a jetport that would have destroyed the Florida
Everglades.
    ISBN 0-8114-7219-1,— ISBN 0-8114-8059-3 (softcover)
    1. Airports—Environmental aspects—Florida—Everglades—
Juvenile literature. 2. Environmental policy—Florida—Everglades—
Citizen participation—Juvenile literature. 3. Environmental protec-
tion—Florida—Everglades—Juvenile literature.[1. Everglades (Fla.)
2. Environmental protection—Florida—Everglades. 3. Airports—
Environmental aspects—Florida—Everglades.] I. Davis, Allen, ill.
II. Title. III. Series
HE9797.5.U52F87 1993
333.91'816'0975939—dc20   92-18085
                                                 CIP
                                                 AC

ISBN 0-8114-7219-1 (Hardcover)
ISBN 0-8114-8059-3 (Softcover)

Introduction
by Alex Haley, General Editor

Life is about choosing. Some choices are simple. Do you brush your teeth before or after you eat breakfast? Do you do your chores before or after your favorite TV show comes on?

But some choices are a lot harder to make than those two. Do you build a factory that will bring jobs to a community even if it also brings pollution and overcrowding? You might say no if you have a job, but yes if you need one. You might say no if you live near the factory, but yes if you own a restaurant nearby where the factory workers will surely eat lunch.

People in communities face choices like this all the time. Often they come into conflict over them. *Save the Everglades* is a story about one such conflict and how it was resolved.

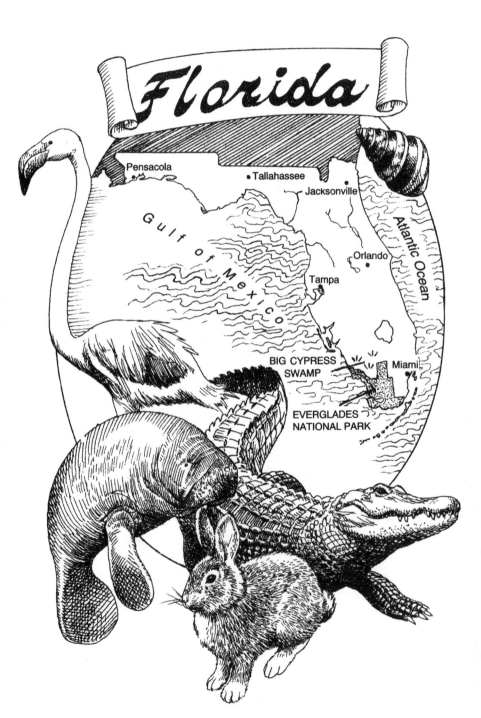

Contents

❋ 1 ❋
In the Swamp

It was a bright Saturday morning in 1969. The sun had peeked up over the Atlantic Ocean at 6:30, flooding the sky with golden light.

Now, a half hour later, Joe Browder was in his car heading west, away from the rising sun. He was driving from the city of Miami to Big Cypress Swamp. Joe's friend Ray was in the front seat beside him. Joe's two sons, Monte and Ron, were in the back. The boys had rolled their windows down all the way so they could feel the cool morning breeze. Sunlight streamed into the car.

Ron was scanning the marsh that lined the road, hoping to spot an alligator in the sawgrass. The boys often saw alligators by the side of the road on their way to Big Cypress Swamp. Sometimes they would get just a glimpse of a grayish green tail as the alligator disappeared into the swamp. But other times they saw two or three alligators lying about with their eyes closed, warming themselves in the sun.

Joe and his sons went out into the wetlands together every Saturday morning. Sometimes they went to Everglades National Park, sometimes to Big Cypress Swamp.

Everglades National Park was huge, covering more than one-and-a-half million acres. It was made up of many different kinds of land, from mangrove swamps to vast expanses of sawgrass. Big Cypress Swamp, on the other hand, was just what the name implied: swampland covered with cypress trees.

Of all the many different places to go inside the Everglades, Monte's particular favorite was Mahogany Hammock. It was an island full of old hardwood trees that were great for climbing. From their branches you could look down upon many huge areas of the park. Monte had never climbed a tree without spotting some animal in the distance. Sometimes he saw white-tailed deer or wild pigs. Several times he had even seen a bobcat. But that was pretty rare. Usually the only animals he could count on seeing were raccoons and possums. And birds, thousands and thousands of them, circling above the treetops or diving down to the water to snatch a fish.

When Monte and Ron had school friends along, they usually went to Mahogany Hammock because it was just a short stroll from where they parked the car. Big Cypress was another story. They didn't often bring friends there. Going into the swamp required wading out into water that was sometimes waist or chest deep. Not everyone wanted to do that. Most people didn't like getting wet.

They didn't like the idea that they might be sharing the water with an alligator. And they didn't like having to circle carefully around old trees, so as not to disturb any sleeping snakes.

Joe turned off the highway and onto a well-worn dirt track. Now they could hear the sounds of the animals just waking in the swamp. Frogs croaked, giving out little whistles or louder bellowing sounds. Birds flying up into the sky chattered and squawked. After driving down the dirt track for about ten minutes, Joe pulled the car onto the side of the road and shut off the engine. Everyone climbed out of the car. Even though they were going wading, they all still wore jeans, T-shirts, and sneakers. Later, when they came out of the swamp, their clothes would dry quickly in the hot noon sun.

Just off the dirt road, the water began. Here it was very shallow, barely up to their ankles. The boys walked behind their father and Ray. Joe warned them to be careful.

Many alligators lived in the swamp, and snakes sunned themselves on cypress "knees"—gnarled roots that stuck up out of the water.

There were plenty of large cypress trees as well. They blocked out some of the sun, providing welcome shade on hot days. But even without the sunlight glistening on it, the water looked clear and fresh. You could see right down to the bottom.

Ray carried a large forked stick and a canvas bag. Today he would be searching for water moccasins. Ray went to a local college. He earned the money to buy his books by catching water moccasins. He took the snakes to a place in Miami where the venom was taken from them. Then the snakes were returned to the swamp. Their venom was used to make medicine to give people who had been bitten by poisonous snakes. On a good morning, Ray might find fifteen or twenty water moccasins.

Joe and Ray moved slowly, scanning the

water and the "knees" for sleeping moccasins. Ray had a good eye. He could spot a snake sunning itself on a cypress knee yards away. Then he would steal up behind it, gliding silently through the water. When he got close enough, he would take his forked stick and quickly place it over the snake. One prong would come down on each side of its body. This trapped the snake on the knee and made it impossible for the snake to move. When Ray was sure that the snake couldn't reach up and bite him, he would grasp it firmly just behind the head and drop it in his bag.

Joe, Monte, and Ron always stayed well away when Ray was catching a snake. They knew that water moccasins were dangerous. Only someone who knew how to handle them could risk trying to catch one.

Ray knew how to handle them. Once he had reached down and caught one that was swimming through the water. He just grasped it behind the head and pulled it out of the water with his bare hands. Joe had been startled, but Ray had calmly dropped the snake in his bag and grinned. He had been catching snakes since he was a boy.

Ray was born in South Florida. He had lived here all his life. The Everglades and Big Cypress Swamp were like home to him. He knew them well.

Joe also knew them well. He hadn't been born in Florida, but he had come to love it as much as Ray did. These Saturday mornings were like heaven to him. He couldn't imagine not being able to come out to Big Cypress Swamp or the Everglades. Monte and Ron loved it out here, too. Joe often thought about what it would be like when they were grown up. He hoped they would be able to bring their children out here every week, too.

As he moved slowly through the water, Joe could hear Monte and Ron splashing behind him. Something didn't seem quite right today but he wasn't sure what it was. He stood perfectly still for a moment, listening to the sounds of Big Cypress around him. He had

been out here earlier in the week. Something was definitely different now.

Then he suddenly realized what it was. He couldn't hear the grinding, crashing sounds of bulldozers at work. Today was Saturday. No one worked the bulldozers on Saturday. It was only when he was out here during the week that he could hear them tearing up Big Cypress Swamp. They were clearing the ground to make room for a jetport. It was going to be the biggest jetport in the world. And when it was finished, Big Cypress Swamp and the Everglades would never be the same again.

✻ 2 ✻
The Biggest Jetport in the World

Joe had first seen the jetport site in Big Cypress Swamp almost a year ago. The bulldozers had been hard at work for almost ten months. Building a jetport in the middle of a swamp was not easy. Trees had to be torn down. Wet ground had to be drained. Land had to be filled in and packed down hard. But the bulldozers were winning the battle. Already, the swamp was beginning to be tamed.

Now a huge sign hung at the entrance to the jetport site. It bragged: "The World's First All-New Jetport for the Supersonic Age." A road led to a two-mile-long landing strip. It was the first of several landing strips to be built. The long strip looked like a black scar carved into the green swamp.

Along both sides of the landing strip, giant machines roared and rumbled like steel dinosaurs, tearing at the earth. Cypress and pondapple trees lay like broken matchsticks. In the distance, cranes cut into limestone pits, gathering landfill. Other large machines spread the limestone fill over the bare, swampy ground. The rock would make the ground hard enough for jets to land on.

The chopped-down trees had once been home to raccoons, possums, and birds. Alligators and snakes had lived on the swampy wetland. Now cranes, bulldozers, and landfill machines were working everywhere. Their angry noises filled the air. No animals could be seen or heard for miles around the swamp.

Before the jetport idea became popular, few people had tried to build in Big Cypress

Swamp. It was one of the few untouched areas of land left in Florida. But progress had come to Big Cypress, just as it had to the rest of the state.

More and more people were moving to Florida and taking over more and more of the natural environment. While Everglades National Park belonged to the nation, Big Cypress was privately owned by Florida businessmen. It could be bought, sold, and developed.

But why was a jetport being built in the middle of a swamp? Didn't anyone care that it was so close to Everglades National Park? The answer to these questions lay in another Florida community. It was the huge, growing community of the city of Miami.

Miami sits on the sandy beaches of the Atlantic Ocean, east of the Everglades. For years, people had been flocking to Miami for its jobs, its beauty, and its warm climate. Joe Browder had himself moved to Miami from Texas. Each year, the Miami International Airport became busier and more crowded.

Finally, the people in charge of the airport knew they had a problem. The airport simply wasn't big enough for Miami's population. It was time to build a bigger and better one. They first had to find a place to build it.

The people of Miami wanted a new airport, but they didn't want to live near it. The noise of huge jets taking off and landing was a headache for everyone. For years, people had complained about the noise. And no one liked the pollution from the jet engines. But there was very little open land left around Miami. Where could an airport be built so people wouldn't be bothered by its noise and pollution?

It seemed that Big Cypress Swamp was the answer. Plenty of land was available there, and it was cheap land. It was far enough away from Miami that noise wouldn't be a problem for people. As one official said, "Nobody will be close enough to complain—except, possibly, alligators."

The idea caught fire. Airlines, businesses, and government leaders started to plan. The

Miami newspapers ran stories with big head-lines: "Plan a New Airport for the Future," "Airport in Glades Can Bring in $$," "Florida's Aviation Future Keyed to Glades Jetport."

The idea kept growing and growing. At first, the Glades jetport was planned just for training flights. Soon, people got bigger ideas. "I have dreams in the sky," said the head of the jetport. "It can develop in the future into the greatest supersonic port in the country." Soon more and more of the swamp was needed for the jetport.

By the time the bulldozers moved in, the jetport was to cover 39 square miles. That was big enough to hold the combined air-ports of four major United States cities!

The jetport would need many buildings and landing strips. Two extra-long runways were planned for supersonic jets. Planes would be taking off or landing every thirty seconds! Terminals, control towers, and hangars would sprawl around the runways.

Parking lots, hotels, gas stations, and restaurants would spring up around the jetport. It would be grand!

The jetport did have one major problem. It was almost fifty miles from Miami. The only road was the Tamiami Trail, which was too narrow for all the traffic that would be coming to the jetport. Again, the planners thought big. The Tamiami Trail, which passed along the northern edge of Everglades National Park, would be widened to handle heavy car traffic. They would also build a "super-train" to carry people to and from Miami. It would whisk passengers along at 250 miles per hour!

The roar of excitement among jetport supporters was almost as loud as a jumbo jet taking off. Jetport planners received the go-ahead from state and federal officials. In October 1968, they broke ground for the jetport in Big Cypress Swamp. In little more than a year, the first jet was to take off!

People who loved the Everglades knew

Lake
Okeechobee

Gulf of
Mexico

Atlantic Ocean

BIG
CYPRESS
SWAMP

Miami
International
Airport

Miccosukee
Land Area

Jetport
Site

Miami

Tamiami
Trail

Everglades
National
Park

N
W   E
S

this was the beginning of the end for the park. They were angry. Building and using the jetport would slowly destroy the natural environment of Big Cypress Swamp. And eventually it would destroy Everglades National Park, too. The park superintendent was asked what the jetport meant for the Everglades. "Slow death," he answered.

Joe Browder and a few other people around Miami raised their voices against the jetport. But they were either ignored or made fun of. Friends of the jetport called them "butterfly chasers" and "birdwatchers."

The head of the jetport joined in the name calling. He thought the "butterfly chasers" were silly to worry about the plants and animals of the Everglades. People could go to the zoo if they wanted to see wild animals. The jetport would mean progress. It would mean jobs.

He wasn't a bit bothered by the protests of the "butterfly chasers" and "birdwatchers." Let them chirp away. The bulldozers worked on, tearing down tree after tree. The landing strip grew longer and longer. The jetport planners thought that once work on the jetport started, it wouldn't be stopped. Joe often wondered if maybe they were right. Maybe nobody could stop the jetport now.

✳ 3 ✳
The People Who Helped

When Joe Browder went out to Big Cypress Swamp with Ray and his sons that day in 1969, he had already been fighting against the jetport for a long time. As head of the Miami chapter of the National Audubon Society, he had been one of the first people to realize the threat the jetport posed to the Everglades.

Joe began the fight by gathering as much local support as he could. Sometimes this wasn't easy. Some people just didn't seem to care one way or the other. Others were strongly in favor of the jetport. One determined politician who wanted the jetport to be built said, "We will be able to do this, no matter what anyone says. There's nothing but alligators out in the Everglades, and alligators can't vote."

Finally, Joe realized that he would need the support of some of the hunters who actually lived in the Everglades. For these people, the destruction of the Everglades meant the end of their way of life. The land would be ruined by polluted water, and the animals they hunted and fished would disappear. Even so, he knew it wouldn't be easy to get them to join the fight against the jetport. Most of them lived in the Everglades because they didn't want other people interfering in their lives. They were the kind of people who didn't like to get involved in anything that was organized or official sounding.

Until 1964, when it became illegal, most of these hunters had made extra money by hunting alligators. Many of them still caught alligators, even though it was now against the

law. They were paid well because the alligator hides were used to make expensive shoes, belts, and bags.

Joe knew that these hunters probably wouldn't want to talk to him. The Audubon Society was one of the groups that tried to stop them from hunting alligators. But he also knew that if the jetport was completed, no one would be able to hunt in the Everglades anymore. He decided that if he could get the hunters to listen, they just might want to join his fight.

First, Joe had to find a way to meet them. They certainly weren't going to come into the Audubon Society office. He mentioned this problem to Ray one day when they were out catching water moccasins. Ray's brother Bruce hunted back in the Everglades. Ray agreed to arrange for Joe to meet him.

The day of the meeting came. Joe drove out to Pine Crest, a small community on the edge of the Everglades. He parked his car in front of the Pine Crest Inn.

As he opened the door of the Pine Crest restaurant, Joe felt a little nervous. He was wearing his Audubon Society shirt. He knew that these people often made fun of those who worked for the Audubon Society. They snickered and called them "birdwatchers," just like the jetport people did. He began to have second thoughts about even trying to talk to them.

Then Joe saw Bruce across the room. He was standing on the edge of the dance floor, one hand thrust into his jean pocket. His hair was combed and slicked back. Joe went over to him. He wanted Bruce to take him around and introduce him to people. He asked if Bruce knew most of the people they saw around them.

"Well, I know a few of these people," Bruce said. "But the person you really want to talk to is over there." He jerked a thumb over his shoulder. "His name is Bill."

Joe looked in the direction Bruce had pointed. He saw a tall man with a craggy, weathered face and twinkling eyes. Bill had hunted so many alligators that people called him Gator Bill. Joe couldn't in a million years imagine someone called Gator Bill being friendly to the head of the Audubon Society.

Still, there was nothing he could do except walk over there and try his luck. This was what he had come to Pine Crest for, after all. He took a breath, walked over to Gator Bill, and stuck out his hand.

"Hi, I'm Joe Browder from the Audubon Society," he said. He waited for Gator Bill to laugh.

And Gator Bill did laugh. The idea of the head of the Audubon Society introducing himself to the top alligator hunter in the Everglades struck Gator Bill as very funny. But his laughter wasn't mean. It was warm and rich, the laughter of a man who enjoyed life.

When Gator Bill had stopped laughing he reached out and shook Joe's hand. They spent the rest of the evening discussing the jetport.

Joe explained how much the Everglades was threatened, and how this would destroy Gator Bill's way of life. He told Gator Bill that the jetport was just the beginning. All of Big Cypress might eventually be developed, polluting Everglades water and scaring away the animals. Gator Bill was convinced. He agreed to gather the other hunters together and join the fight.

A few weeks later, Joe went to see Buffalo Tiger. Buffalo Tiger was the chief of the Miccosukee Indians. The Miccosukee had been living in the Everglades for over two hundred years. At first some of the Miccosukee had supported the jetport because the jetport planners had promised them jobs. But now the bulldozers had razed Green Corn Hammock. This was an island where the Miccosukee performed one of their sacred ceremonies, the Green Corn Ritual. Joe knew they were angry about that. He also knew that they hadn't gotten as many jobs as they had been promised.

Joe went out to an island in the Everglades where some of the Miccosukee lived. He met with Buffalo Tiger. He explained that the noise of the jets would go on around the clock. Traffic and pollution would change their tribal lands forever. Big Cypress would be developed and the Miccosukee would be pushed out. Buffalo Tiger held a meeting with the Miccosukee council. They decided that the Miccosukee must join the fight.

Joe also enlisted the help of many young people from Miami. Charles Lee, December Duke, and other high school students would come to the Audubon office and plan how they could help. They designed posters and signs to put up in their schools, where they gave talks about the Everglades. They distributed bumper stickers that said SAVE THE GLADES—STOP THE JETPORT. They mailed letters around the country, asking people to join the fight against the jetport.

Joe had done a lot to organize people against the jetport. For over a year now, he had been guiding the fight to save the Everglades and Big Cypress Swamp. He had made a lot of people angry. They were afraid that if Joe stopped the jetport they would lose a lot of money. There were even signs posted around town that read: "WANTED: Joe Browder. God will reward any man who accidentally happens to shoot him." But Joe still felt that the opposition to the jetport wasn't strong enough. He needed someone famous to work with them—someone people would listen to. He decided to go and talk to Marjory Stoneman Douglas.

Years before, Mrs. Douglas had written a best-selling book about the Everglades called *River of Grass*. She was famous and she had helped make the Everglades famous. Joe hoped that if she joined the fight more people would listen to what the jetport opposition had to say.

❋ 4 ❋
Mrs. Douglas

One day Joe Browder drove out to a small house in Coconut Grove, one of the greenest and prettiest areas of Miami.

Mrs. Douglas knew Joe Browder because he was the head of the Miami Audubon Society. They had even met a few times. In fact, just the day before she had mentioned to a friend that she thought he was doing good work in his fight against the jetport. And now here he was on her doorstep. Mrs. Douglas invited him into the house.

Mrs. Douglas's house was filled with books. Joe saw books on the table, on chairs, even stacked on the floor. Mrs. Douglas was busy trying to write another book of her own, and she needed all these other books for research. As he sat down on her comfortable sofa, Joe marveled at how such a tiny, seventy-eight-year-old woman could still have so much energy.

Mrs. Douglas made tea, which she served from a beautiful china teapot. They sat with their cups for a while in silence. They both knew why Joe had come, but for the moment it was nice just to sit and not think about the jetport.

Finally, though, Joe put down his cup and began to talk. He explained that he needed her help in the fight against the jetport. He brought up her book on the Everglades and how well-known she was. He knew how much she loved the park. He said, "If the jetport is built and the land is drained, the water for the Everglades will be polluted. Wildlife will disappear. You are more famous than anyone. People will respect you. They will listen to you."

Mrs. Douglas smiled. "Just because I wrote a book doesn't mean they'll listen to me. I'm just one person. People don't listen to one person about anything. They listen to organizations."

Now it was Joe's turn to smile. "So why don't you start an organization?" he asked.

Mrs. Douglas didn't have anything to say to that. She knew he was right. She could start an organization if she wanted to help.

But Joe wasn't taking any chances. He decided to take her out to Big Cypress Swamp. He wanted her to see the destruction the jetport had already caused.

They got into his car and drove west along the Tamiami Trail. On the way they talked about the jetport. Joe told her about what had already been done to try to stop it.

The Tamiami Trail runs through the Everglades on its way to Big Cypress Swamp. As they drove through the park the sweet sounds of mockingbirds and wrens filled the air. Mrs. Douglas spotted an otter playing in the canal along the side of the road. It slid down the side of the canal and then floated on its back, basking in the warm sunshine.

As they listened to the birds and watched the otter they grew quiet. Each of them was reminded once again of how much there was to love about the park. They knew it would be destroyed if the jetport was built.

Joe knew from her silence that Mrs. Douglas had already decided to help. But he still wanted her to see what the jetport builders had done.

The jetport was located just beyond a newly constructed dam. This dam was already threatening the Everglades by reducing the flow of water into the park. All the living things in the park depended upon that water. Less water meant fewer living things. Joe drove across the dam so that Mrs. Douglas could get a good look at it.

At last, they reached the jetport site. Joe led Mrs. Douglas to the place where the airstrip was being built. She looked around at the fallen trees and the bald patches of

land. She saw the swampland torn apart and drained.

That's all it took. Mrs. Douglas could see that the jetport would destroy much of Big Cypress Swamp. And she knew it was too close to the Everglades not to affect that park as well. She promised Joe she would help him in the fight against the jetport.

Back in Miami, Mrs. Douglas brooded over how best to help. What could she do? At a picnic one afternoon, she was talking to a young person concerned about the Everglades. Mrs. Douglas was toying with an idea but it seemed too simple to be good.

"What would you think," she said, trying the idea out on the young man, "about joining an organization called something like The Friends of the Everglades? We'd make it so that anybody could join for, say, a dollar."

Mrs. Douglas didn't just want to know if he thought it was a good idea. She was also wondering if he thought it would make a difference. The young man looked at her and then reached into his pocket and pulled out a dollar bill.

"I think," he said, "it's a great idea."

The young man and his dollar were just the beginning. Wearing a flowery dress and a big, floppy hat, Mrs. Douglas made speeches all over Florida. She always spoke her mind, plainly and strongly, in a way that won people over. Young and old, people paid their dollars and joined The Friends of the Everglades.

In her speeches Mrs. Douglas told people how the jetport would hurt the Everglades. The park would be spoiled, she told them, and not just for its wildlife. People went to the Everglades to be in the wilderness. If the wilderness was harmed, people wouldn't come.

Instead of the sounds of birds and animals, people would hear the rumble and roar of jumbo jets taking off. Every ninety seconds a plane would take off or land. The pollution would drive many of the swamp animals away from the jetport. And it wasn't just air and noise pollution either. Mrs. Douglas explained how the water in the swamp would be ruined and how that would affect the water in the Everglades. Fresh water comes to Everglades National Park from the north. It passes through Big Cypress Swamp. The jetport would sit in the middle of the flow of fresh water. The water flowing into the Everglades would carry the jetport pollution with it.

Mrs. Douglas said the people of Florida had to make a choice. They could have the jetport. Or they could have the Everglades. But they couldn't have both at the same time, so close together.

🌴

The jetport had begun as a local problem, but Joe, Mrs. Douglas, and the others worked hard to get the whole nation involved. After all, the Everglades was a national park. It belonged to all Americans.

Joe and Mrs. Douglas began to get more help from people all over the country. These people belonged to groups interested in wildlife, the environment, and the national parks. Working alone, people had little power to stop the bulldozers. But together they were being heard over the grinding roar of the heavy machines.

The fight over the jetport even had people in Washington, D.C., involved. The Secretary of Transportation, John A. Volpe, was a strong supporter of the jetport. To counteract Volpe's support, those fighting the jetport tried to get the Secretary of the Interior, Walter J. Hickel, on their side. They argued that Everglades park was a national treasure. It had to be saved!

Secretary Hickel listened to their arguments. Then he said he needed more facts about the jetport and how it would affect the Everglades. He ordered a long careful study to be made. Now the Friends of the Everglades knew they had a chance. The facts were on their side. They were sure of that. But they weren't sure that the study would be completed in time to stop the jetport.

✳ 5 ✳
Victory!

Joe Browder sat in a chair in the White House conference room. He was meeting with President Richard Nixon's environmental advisor. The advisor sat across from him, on the other side of a big oval table.

Joe had picked the chair he sat in very carefully. It was the President's chair, the one the President used when he met with his advisors. There was a legend about this chair. Anyone who sat in it could make one wish and it would come true. Joe closed his eyes and wished for the President to stop the jetport.

For a while now, things had been going

very well in the fight against the jetport. Joe thought back on all that had happened since Secretary Hickel had become interested in the fight. The scientists Hickel hired had completed their study and presented it to him.

The things they learned were not good. They discovered that exhaust from the jets would harm the birds that might fly into it. They also discovered that a jet plane spews out one gallon of unburned fuel at take-off. If a jet took off every minute or two, there would be a huge amount of fuel spewed out every day. That fuel would become a poison rain falling into the Everglades. Worst of all, the exhaust from the jets and the poisons used to keep the area free of mosquitoes would eventually enter the water supply of the Everglades. This would endanger all the wildlife, because every living creature needs clean water to survive.

The scientists had determined that the jetport must be stopped. When Secretary Hickel

heard their report, he agreed. He met with Secretary Volpe and showed him the report. He explained that the scientists had decided the jetport was a bad idea. But Secretary Volpe wouldn't change his mind. He still thought the jetport was a good idea. It meant America would have the most advanced airport in the world. And it would give the people of Miami more jobs.

The two secretaries continued to be on opposite sides of the jetport battle. Their disagreement finally reached the ears of President Nixon. He talked to Secretary Hickel and Secretary Volpe. To the President, both men seemed to have very good arguments. He didn't know what to do. He decided he wanted to learn more about the jetport.

But President Nixon was a very busy man. He needed someone who could go to Florida and report back to him about what was happening to the Everglades.

That's why Joe was meeting with the President's environmental advisor. President

Nixon had asked his daughter, Julie Nixon, to go down to Florida for him. Now Joe and the environmental advisor were planning the trip. Joe wanted to make sure that Julie Nixon saw the beauty of the Everglades. He wanted her to understand why people loved these wetlands so much. Then maybe her report, along with Secretary Hickel's, would convince the President to stop the jetport.

When all the plans for the trip were complete, Joe returned to Florida. As his plane landed in Miami, he looked out the window. The city lay sprawled beneath him. He wondered what it would be like to land in the middle of Big Cypress Swamp. He hoped that he would never have to find out.

Joe and his friends worked hard to get ready for Julie Nixon's visit. Secret Service agents came down to Florida. It was their job to make sure Julie Nixon would be safe. They hired Gator Bill as a guide. One of his tasks was to walk ahead of Julie Nixon and catch any water moccasins that might be laying on the trail. Moccasins could be dangerous if they were startled. And no one wanted Julie Nixon to have a showdown with a startled moccasin.

Julie Nixon flew down to Miami and went out to the Everglades. She walked along the trails and saw deer and alligators and otters. She saw a flock of ibis rise up from underneath an ancient cypress tree. She saw hundreds of orchids and other beautiful flowers growing wild.

Julie Nixon went back to the White House and told the President that the Everglades was indeed a national treasure. She had seen its beauty for herself. She recommended that the jetport be stopped.

President Nixon listened to his daughter. He reviewed the reports of his secretaries. Then he made his decision.

The President called a press conference. He announced that he was against the jetport. He ordered Miami to find a new jetport site. The Everglades would be saved after all.

The jetport planners knew that they had lost. Only a year before, they were sure of getting their way. They had said only alligators would complain about the jetport. Now even the President had decided they were wrong.

Government leaders in Florida and in Miami's Dade County took a new look at the jetport plans. They decided to solve the airport problem in a different way. In January 1970, they signed an agreement with the United States government. They promised to search for a new airport site. They also promised that the new plans would not harm the Everglades. The one runway built in Big Cypress Swamp was allowed to remain for training flights.

After the President's decision, Joe took Monte and Ron out to Mahogany Hammock one beautiful afternoon. The boys climbed the trees while Joe rested in the shade of an ancient mahogany. He could hear the quiet murmur of their voices as they whispered to

each other about the animals they had spotted. Joe felt an overwhelming sense of peace.

Big Cypress Swamp had been saved. Monte and Ron could still see wildlife from the trees. The animals hadn't been destroyed or driven away. But Joe knew that the fight was not completely over. He would have to fight to save the Everglades for the rest of his life.

Then Joe thought of Marjory Douglas. He hoped that when he turned eighty he would have the same strength and determination to fight for the things he loved. Sitting under this tree, watching a great blue heron search the water for fish, Joe felt willing to fight forever. He closed his eyes, stretched out his legs, and waited for the boys to come down from the trees.

✴ Epilogue ✴

The battle to save the Everglades didn't end after the victory against the jetport. From 1969 until the present, people have been working tirelessly to make sure that Everglades Park stays a national treasure.

Many of the people who fought against the jetport worked hard to convince the government to buy Big Cypress Swamp. They realized that as long as the swamp was privately owned, it could be built on and polluted. They wanted the government to buy it so this could never happen. In 1974, the government finally bought Big Cypress Swamp.

They changed its name to Big Cypress Preserve. Now it belongs to the nation.

The Everglades' water supply was also in great danger. As more people moved to South Florida, more land was drained and cleared. More pesticides and fertilizers were used. More sewage was dumped. All of these things posed a threat to the park's water supply. At the end of 1989, President George Bush signed a bill to add over one hundred thousand acres to the park. This area, called the East Everglades, was set aside to protect the park's water supply.

Like the Everglades' water supply, its animals were also in danger. The growing number of people in Florida was crowding them out. The panther was a good example. Although it was Florida's state animal, less than fifty of them were still alive. At the age of ninety-eight, Marjory Stoneman Douglas took up the cause of the Florida panther. She traveled the state asking people to help her fight to save it. She helped people realize how much danger the panther was in.

The fight against the jetport also changed the lives of many of the participants. Gator Bill and his friends never went back to hunting alligators. They realized that killing too many alligators might alter the Everglades for good. They knew they wanted to protect the park, not help destroy it.

Charles Lee, one of the students who joined the fight, grew up to become vice president of the Florida Audubon Society. He still works every day to protect wildlife and nature.

The fight against the jetport was the first environmental fight of its kind. People realized that by working together they could save an endangered area. Since 1969 many people have organized fights to save the lands they love. The battle to save threatened lands and animals will always go on. Perhaps one day it will be your turn to fight.

Afterword

This book tells the story of a struggle that happened more than twenty years ago. All the people mentioned in the book are real. All the events described really happened. The information was taken from newspaper and magazine articles, Marjory Stoneman Douglas's autobiography, and interviews with Joe Browder. All the conversations shown in quotation marks are exact or almost exact quotes. Some details—the splash of an alligator's tail or the way the wind or sunlight streamed through an open car window—were imagined to complete a scene or set a mood.

Special thanks are extended to Joe Browder for his time and interest in the Everglades and in this story. We would also like to thank James Webb, Florida Regional Director of the Wilderness Society, for reading early drafts of this work. A debt of gratitude is owed to Sunita Apte for her interviews with Joe Browder and her work on the chapters involving him in the text.

Notes

Page 2 The Everglades is one of the largest wetlands in the world. It stretches over 2,746 square miles, from Lake Okeechobee in the north to the Bay of Florida in the south and the Gulf of Mexico in the west. Everglades National Park is only a small part of this wetlands. This part became a national park in 1947.

Page 22 The American alligator lives in various parts of the southeastern United States. It is closely related to the crocodile. Alligators were once very plentiful in the Florida wetlands. But over the years, a large number of them were killed for their valuable hides. They became scarce.

In 1967 the alligator was named an endangered species. This meant that alligators were protected by the government because they were in danger of completely dying out. No one was allowed to hunt them. By 1977, however, the alligator population had grown enough that hunting on a limited basis was once again allowed.

Page 39 The Everglades study was done by a scientist named Art Marshall. Marshall worked for the United States Fish and Wildlife Service and knew a lot about the Everglades. Even after the jetport fight, he continued to try to help the Everglades. One of the most beautiful places in the Everglades was named in his honor. The Arthur A. Marshall Loxahatchee National Wildlife Refuge is north of Everglades National Park.

Page 50 The law that made Big Cypress Swamp into Big Cypress Preserve also helped the Miccosukee Indians. The law stated that the Miccosukee would always be able to live in the preserve. No one could stop them from hunting, fishing, and carrying out their Green Corn Dance and other sacred rituals within the preserve.

Judith Bauer Stamper is a writer and editor. In addition to her nonfiction work, she is the author of several best-selling collections of short stories for children.